COCKTAILS
and After Dinner Drinks

David Biggs

Photography by Ryno Reyneke

COCKTAILS
and After Dinner Drinks

NEW
HOLLAND

This edition published in 2006

First published in 2005 by New Holland Publishers (UK) Ltd
London Cape Town Sydney Auckland

Garfield House, 86–88 Edgware Road, London W2 2EA, United Kingdom
www.newhollandpublishers.com

80 McKenzie Street, Cape Town 8001, South Africa

Level 1, Unit 4, 14 Aquatic Drive, Frenchs Forest, NSW 2086, Australia

218 Lake Road, Northcote, Auckland, New Zealand

ISBN-10: 1 84537 680 3
ISBN-13: 978 1 84537 680 2

Publishing managers: Claudia Dos Santos, Simon Pooley
Commissioning editor: Alfred LeMaitre
Editor: Katja Splettstoesser
Designer: Petaldesign
Stylist: Anke Roux
Proofreader: Gill Gordon
Picture researcher: Tamlyn McGeean, Karla Kik
Production: Myrna Collins

10 9 8 7 6 5 4 3 2 1

Printed and bound by Tien Wah Press, Malaysia

contents

Man's ingenious spirit has driven him to create a whole world of alcoholic drinks, each suited to a particular occasion or event. There are times when we drink to quench a thirst, or to sharpen our tastebuds before a meal, or to toast a friend or a special occasion. Wine goes with food, beer goes with thirst and champagne goes with celebration and the last drink of the day—the one we have after dinner and before going to bed—is drunk for no

prologue

other reason than sheer pleasure. It allows us to retire with a feeling of warm contentment and relaxation.

Late-night cocktails may take many forms, according to local custom or family tradition. In Scotland it would probably consist of a sip of well-aged single malt whisky, while the traditional after-dinner drink in England is an aged port. The French appreciate a bedtime balloon glass of good Cognac and South Africans enjoy a fine pot-still brandy or a sweet jerepigo. In each case the drink is designed to help you digest your meal and wash away the cares of the world. No wonder it is sometimes referred to as a nightcap.

Ideally your cocktail should be a short drink, because a longer one—a beer for example—will have you up for a bathroom break or two during the night. This is not a time for quenching thirsts. It's a time for lingering tastes. Your nightcap should also be relatively high in alcohol because alcohol has a soothing, soporific effect, and of course, the drink should taste and smell warm and inviting. Interestingly, late-night drinks are usually dark in color—note the deep ruby or amber of a good port, for example, or the rich old gold of a fine cognac or whisky, rather than the silver clarity of a gin or vodka. White spirit drinks suit the daytime, while evening and darkness call for drinks that are equally dark. There are exceptions, of course, and you'll find many drinkers from northern lands retire after a glass of vodka, schnapps, or *akvavit*.

In this little book we take a look at some of our choices, for there are many.

A WELL-PLANNED DINNER
SHOULD APPEAR TO BE EFFORTLESS.

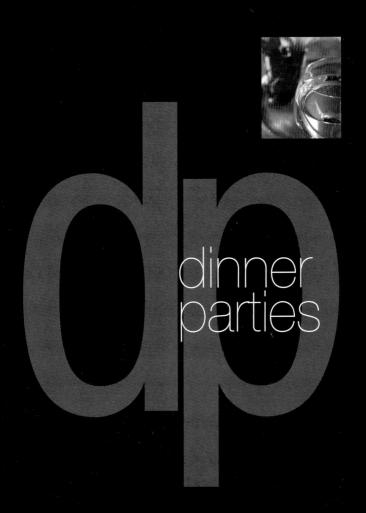

dinner
parties

A cocktail can mean different things at different times. It all depends, of course, on the form the evening takes. Having guests for dinner could be anything from an intimate candlelit meal for two to an elaborate five-course anniversary banquet for 20 guests. Whatever shape it takes, a good dinner needs careful planning if it is to be a success. Not many of us can afford a team of waiters. In today's lifestyle we have to do most of the work ourselves, Remember, though, that the essence of a good meal is in the company, rather than the food. A simple meal with good company and interesting conversation is far more rewarding than the elaborate performance of a gourmet that prevents a relaxed chat.

"I have drunk my wine with my milk; eat,
O friends; drink, yes drink
abundantly O Beloved."
King Solomon

Preparation

When planning a dinner party decide in advance what you intend to serve at each stage of the dinner and make sure you have the necessary ingredients. One of the essential tools for a great evening is a hot tray or bain-marie on which the food can be kept hot next to the table until it is needed. The food can then be served with a minimum of fuss when required, and without the host having to leave the scene. Dinner planners might find it useful to have a checklist list handy when organizing their event. This preparation goes as much for the drinks as for the food. No matter what drinks you choose to serve, and at what stage of the evening, attention to detail makes all the difference.

If there is to be a welcoming glass of champagne to greet your guests, ensure that there are glasses ready and that the bottle is resting in an ice-bucket, ready to be popped. If sherry is served with the soup, see that there's a sherry glass at each guest's place. On a hot evening sherry is traditionally served lightly chilled.

The wines to go with each course should be opened and nearby for effortless pouring. Red wine could be opened a few hours before the first guests arrive; white wines opened and chilled. This way you can avoid any embarrassing breaks in conversation caused by you wrestling with a reluctant cork.

Most guests like to sip iced water with their meals, partly to clear the palate between courses and also to dilute the effects of wine before the return journey afterwards. You can serve the iced water in an elegant glass pitcher (maybe with ice and a slice or two of lemon) or even offer bottled still or sparkling mineral water that has been well chilled before the time.

One problem that must be solved in your own way is exactly how many glasses to provide for each guest. If you try provide a sherry, white wine, red wine, and water glass for each place setting you could end up with a hopelessly cluttered table (unless yours is very large).

A drinks trolley drawn up next to the table might help to solve this, or have the red wine glasses ready on a tray, to be distributed after the sherry.

Draw up your plan to suit your circumstances. The key to it all is to ensure as little disruption as possible. Serving coffee afterwards? Have it laid out all ready on a trolley, so you can switch on the percolator and wheel it all in. When it all looks effortless, your guests will feel more relaxed.

A welcoming drink puts everybody in a party mood.

The welcoming drink

Guests seldom arrive all at the same time, so it eases them into the evening if they are offered a welcoming drink upon arrival. One of the reasons for doing this is to prevent them from standing around empty-handed, wondering whether they came too early.

Traditionally, the welcoming drink used to be a tiny glass of dry sherry, and this is still a good way to begin an evening. There are several styles of sherry, making it an exceptionally versatile drink. Among them Amontillado—a fino that is aged until it has lost its clean, elegant character but developed a nutty flavor that is charming in itself. Then there's Amoroso, which is basically an Oloroso sherry that has been slightly sweetened to suit the English palate.

The more modern trend in welcoming drinks, however, is to start the evening with a glass of brut sparkling wine. Early arrivals can stand sipping and getting into party mood while waiting for the latecomers.

In preparation for the perfect welcoming cocktail on a summer evening, set out as many champagne flutes as the number of expected guests a hour before your guests arrive. Into each one place a slice of fresh, soft fruit. (Peaches are perfect, as are strawberries, plums, or large, seedless grapes cut in halves.) Cover each fruit slice with brandy and leave to stand so the fruit can absorb the brandy flavor.

Shortly before the guests are due to arrive, half-fill each glass with fruit juice—orange or mango are perfect for this, as are fruit-juice blends. When your first guests arrive, open a chilled bottle of dry sparkling wine and top up each guest's glass as you hand it to them. They'll feel very welcome.

You could also prepare a welcoming punch bowl in advance. As each guest arrives he or she can be handed a glass. It's quick and elegant. You could, for example, greet each guest with a Champagne Cup (see p26). When soft fruit is in season you may like to make use of it and prepare a

SHERRY

Sherry has been around for many centuries.
The Shakespearean name for it was *Sherris Sack*, which is actually closer
to its real name (Jerez) than our modern one. The 'Sack' part
of it was the Anglicized form of the Spanish word 'seco',
used to describe a dry, fortified wine.
Several other countries have produced what they claim to be sherry,
but a historic international court case in Spain in 1968 ruled that
only the fortified wine of Andalusia could be called sherry.
Anything else had to be labelled as Australian Sherry or
South African Sherry, for example.
More recently the EU has been stricter and the word 'sherry'
is now restricted exclusively to the product of Andalusia.
Others can call their products 'fino' or 'medium cream',
as long as they omit the actual S-word.

summer Peach Bowl (*see* p29). Then there's the Wine Cup (see p30), which makes a crisp and delightful starting drink.

In winter you might like to greet your guests with a hot punch. Hot punch is a variation on the traditional Glühwein recipe known to warm drinkers in northern European countries after a day of skiing. Create your own versions by trial and error—the errors can be pleasant! A good rule to remember when making punch is that wine and brandy are made from grapes, and they combine well with fruits or fruit juices. Grain-based drinks, such as whisky, beer and vodka, sometimes form an uneasy alliance with grape products, and are best avoided.

The main meal

Have you selected a good wine to accompany the main course? Traditions have relaxed in modern times, but it is still safe to serve red wine with red meat and white wine with white meat or fish. Unless you're very sure of yourself, it's preferable to stick to the rule. As a rough guide to the sort of wines that have been found to be a good match for various foods, here's a list of suggestions. Remember they are just that. Suggestions. Feel free to use your imagination.

Soup — a dry sherry or a crisp brut sparkling wine would be ideal.

Fish — a fried fish dish is often teamed with a crisp dry, slightly acid white wine to keep the palate fresh. A Portuguese Vinho Verde is perfect here. When cooking a drier fish dish that is grilled or baked, a fruity Sauvignon blanc would be perfect.

Roast beef — usually a robust, full-flavored red wine, like a Cabernet sauvignon or Bordeaux blend would make a good match.

Roast mutton — this is a full-flavored meat, so it could be teamed with an earthy Pinot noir or a full-bodied Shiraz.

Roast lamb — we're getting into subtleties here. You may like to team the lamb with a dry rosé wine, or a very light-bodied red blend.

Pork — traditionally served with a fruit accompaniment, pork can be successfully matched with an off-dry white wine or a sweetish rosé.

Duck — I'd suggest a Chardonnay here, unwooded if possible, because you'd get more of the citrus character of the wine coming through, and duck traditionally goes well with orange sauce.

Grilled chicken — almost any good white wine is fine here, depending on the flavoring you've added to the chicken. A Sauvignon blanc is good with a mildly flavored dish, while a Gewürztraminer could be perfect with a lightly curried chicken.

Pasta (meat sauce) — obviously a robust Italian-style wine is good here — a Chianti if you can get it.

Pasta (cheese sauce) — cheese varies, so you need to be careful here. A light-bodied red wine should fit the bill.

Curries — these are tricky and often not served with wine at all, but a fruity, semi-sweet white wine often goes very well with a curry. Try a fragrant Gewürztraminer. If your guests are beer drinkers, serve beer, particularly if you're making a robust, hot curry.

Pudding — you do not need to serve a different wine with every course, but it's often pleasant to serve guests a small glass of fortified wine with the pudding. This could be either a Noble Late Harvest wine, or a Canadian ice wine.

Cheese — a sweet wine is the traditional accompaniment to cheese. You could safely serve a Madeira or a Ruby Port.

Coffee — traditionally coffee is served with a good brandy or port. Some hosts, particularly those with Italian backgrounds, like to add a dash of grappa or brandy to the coffee.

Coffee

This brings us to the often-vexed subject of the serving of coffee after a good meal. It often puzzles me why so few restaurants serve good coffee. They go to great lengths to provide an impressive and imaginative menu and then end up with a cup of weak, very indifferent, flavored coffee, and patrons leave the establishment feeling just a little disappointed. A really good cup of coffee, on the other hand, could have sent them on their way with their tastebuds singing.

Just as a coffee maker is a good investment for a restaurateur, so too is it for the home entertainer, whether it's a complicated espresso machine or a simple plunge-pot. Buy various kinds of coffee until you discover the one that suits your own taste. Remember — this will be the flavor lingering in your guests' mouths when they set off for home.

Finally...

We come to that last drink before the party ends. In fact, that last drink can be a useful signal for the party to end.

When guests have reached the stage of wondering whether

it would be polite to leave, the host could announce something like: "Friends, before you set off, how about a small drink for the road." Anybody who doesn't take the hint shouldn't be invited next time.

Remember, though, authorities everywhere are clamping down on drinking and driving. It's very irresponsible to ply your guests with drinks and then send them off to drive home. A part of your dinner planning could be to arrange in advance for a driver to collect your guests and their cars, and ferry them home. Now that would be real style! Alternatively, suggest your guests stay over at your house and travel home the following morning. Obviously this depends on your accommodation.

Included on the following pages are a few recipes for welcoming drinks. They are easy to prepare and will kick-start any party, whether you are having a formal dinner party or a casual get-together.

When it comes to 'one for the road' the safest drink is a cup of strong coffee.

- ✦ Bottle of champagne or dry sparkling wine

- ✦ Half a cup of sherry

- ✦ A quarter cup of brandy

- ✦ A tablespoon of Cointreau

- ✦ Two teaspoons of honey

- ✦ Small chunks of fresh pineapple and orange

Champagne Cup

Take a large glass pitcher and pour in a bottle of well chilled champagne or dry sparkling wine, and add the sherry, brandy and Cointreau.

Add the honey and fresh pineapple and orange chunks. Stir gently to avoid losing the bubbles, and decorate with a sprig of mint.

Now all you have to do is greet your guests and hand each of them a glass of freshly poured punch.

✦ Six very ripe peaches

✦ Three bottles of chilled champagne
   or dry sparkling wine

✦ Half a cup of brandy

✦ Sugar to taste

Peach Bowl

Before the guests arrive prepare for this delicious
drink by peeling the peaches, cutting them into
slices and leaving them to steep in the brandy.

Place the peach slices in a large punch bowl, sprinkle
with sugar, add the brandy, and leave to stand until just
before the guests arrive.

When the first guests arrive, pour the champagne
into the bowl and ladle a helping into each glass or
champagne flute.

- ✦ A bottle of chilled dry white wine

- ✦ Half a cup of diced fresh pineapple

- ✦ Peel of half an orange cut into strips

- ✦ Half a cup of medium cream sherry

- ✦ 1 quart of soda water

- ✦ Ice

Wine Cup

Pour chilled dry white wine into a tall pitcher with the diced
fresh pineapple, orange peel and medium-cream sherry.
Allow the mixture to stand until needed, then top up the
pitcher with soda water, stir gently, and serve with ice.

- ✦ One and a half cups of apple juice
- ✦ Three slices of lemon
- ✦ Four tablespoons of honey
- ✦ A few cloves
- ✦ A small stick of cinnamon
- ✦ A bottle of full-bodied red wine

Hot Burgundy Punch

Place the apple juice, lemon, honey, cloves, and cinnamon stick in a saucepan and bring to the boil, stirring occasionally. When the mixture has boiled for a couple of minutes, add the red wine and reheat, but do not boil this time.

Strain into an insulated pitcher and serve in warmed mugs or wine glasses.

port

THOSE WHO LIVE WELL OFTEN ENJOY A GLASS OF GOOD PORT AFTER A MEAL.

Port is a traditional after-dinner drink and has a fascinating history, linking Britain and Portugal in a unique partnership. Although port is made in the upper reaches of the Douro Valley in Portugal, it was the English who 'discovered' it and developed the port industry. Other countries have made port-style wines, but the Portuguese are guarded about the name and refuse to allow it to be given to any such wine that does not originate in Portugal. The high alcohol content of port, which derives from the addition of brandy to the wine (usually red), ensures that it will last for many years without losing its charm.

> "The gentleman did like a drop too much –
> more Port than was exactly portable."
> Thomas Hood

Port's profile

Port comes in a variety of styles, including Ruby port, Vintage port, Tawny port, Crusted port, Late Bottled Vintage, and even White port. Port is usually made from grape varieties that have proved themselves suitable for this style of wine, with romantic names like Tinta Rouriz, Tinta Barocca, Touriga Naçionale, and Souzao. All are full-bodied grapes capable of producing wines with deep color and full flavors.

Vintage port

When a port producer considers the year to be a particularly excellent one, he may declare it a vintage year. By doing this he is declaring that he considers it better than average and, of course, is putting his reputation on the line. Vintage years are not declared lightly.

Ruby port

This is produced when the port is still young and has a bright ruby color. It is rich and fruity in character, rather like a fine plum pudding.

Tawny port

This is an aged port that has been kept until much of the red pigment has been precipitated, leaving the wine a pale amber color. Some fruitiness will have been lost in the ageing process, but the wine will have replaced this with an understated gentleness.

Late Bottled Vintage

This is port that has been allowed to mature in wooden casks for more years than usual before being bottled. It bears the year of harvest, but has been aged considerably before bottling, picking up more of the old oak flavors and warmth. Usually a complex drink

Some port is matured in oak casks for many years before being bottled.

Crusted port

This is a blended port that is bottled after two years in the barrel. It is similar to a vintage port, but needs to be laid down to mature for some time, to allow it to create a 'crust' or sediment in the bottle. Care is taken when pouring this wine, so the sediment remains in the bottle.

Paraphernalia

Because port is traditionally kept for a long time in the bottle, and often develops sediment, there are several ingenious devices designed to enable the drinker to pour it very gently and without shaking the bottle.

One of these rather complicated devices is the port tilter, that consists of a cradle to hold the bottle, and a cranked tilting mechanism to slowly tip the bottle over, allowing a small amount of port to be poured at a time.

Port is an ancient drink with its own set of traditions and old customs.

Sometimes, a pair of port tongs is used in conjunction with the tilter. Obviously a delicate bottle of very old port needs to be handled gently and the action of inserting a corkscrew and giving it a tug would simply stir up the contents. To prevent this, a pair of special tongs is heated until red hot and clamped round the neck of the bottle, already resting in the cradle of the tilter. Once the neck has been heated a wet feather is stroked across the hot area to cause the neck to crack and break off neatly.

It might all sound like a devil of a palaver just to get a drink, but the anticipation and suspense is well worth it. After all, the last drink of the day is not to be hurried. It is all about gentle, civilized pleasure.

Port goes modern

Just when we thought port was gaining a rather fusty image as the drink of grumpy, red-faced old men with gout, the drink has done a dramatic turnabout and has emerged as the trendy tipple of the young. Another surprising fact is that almost half the port drinkers in Britain today are women.

What's more, a quarter of all the port drunk in Britain is consumed by men and women under the age of 35. This is indeed good news, as it means that old stereotypes are being destroyed and we can drink what we enjoy without fear of being labelled. I am told that other drinks that are increasing in popularity after a slump include sherry, vermouth, and cognac. Let's hope this means drinkers have finally matured to the point where they feel free to drink what pleases their palates, rather than follow fashions.

- ◆ Three parts ruby port
- ◆ One part brandy
- ◆ One egg yolk
- ◆ One teaspoon superfine sugar
- ◆ Grated nutmeg
- ◆ Cream (optional)
- ◆ Ice cubes

Port Flip

Traditionally port has been used in many old family recipes. A Port Flip, for example, is regarded as an excellent reviver of flagging spirits. There's nothing like it for warding off the winter chill after a day outdoors in the mist and sleet.

Place three cubes of ice in a cocktail shaker and add the superfine sugar, egg yolk, port, and brandy.
Shake well and strain into a cocktail or wine glass and add a sprinkling of nutmeg. Float a little cream on top for an even richer drink. See? You're feeling better already.

- ✦ A generous splash of port
- ✦ A little cognac
- ✦ Ice
- ✦ Orange zest

Port Cocktail

Combine the port and cognac.

Stir ingredients with ice and strain into a cocktail glass.

What you're doing here is simply adding extra fortification to the port, which is, after all, wine fortified with brandy.

Top the mixture with a squeeze of orange zest.

- ✦ A measure of port
- ✦ Two measures of lemonade
- ✦ Ice
- ✦ A slice of lemon

Port and Lemon

When I started discovering alcoholic beverages in my late teens, I was introduced to this delightful drink—light and sweet enough to be enjoyed by a very young palate, but just sophisticated enough not to be thought of as a child's drink.

Combine the port and lemonade.
Stir with ice and strain into a cocktail glass.
Garnish with a slice of lemon.

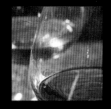

10

brandy

The story of brandy goes back centuries to the time when alchemists first distilled wine in an effort to obtain the elusive 'elixir of life'—the spirit that would keep men young forever. Today a similar distillation is still called *eau de vie*, or the 'water of life'.

Producers have learned that ageing brandy in casks gives it elegance and smoothness. Each brandy-producing country has its own laws regarding the making of this fine spirit. In South Africa, for example, where brandy is the most popular spirit drink of all, at least one-third of the brandy is made by the traditional pot-still method and aged in barrels for at least three years.

"Claret is the liquor for boys,
port for men. But he who aspires
to be a hero must drink brandy."

anon

Brandy's many faces

Brandies come in many guises and all have their place in the market, depending on the way you prefer to serve them. Very often, brandy is used as the base of a long drink, like the classic 'horse's neck' which is brandy mixed with ginger ale. In this case, the flavor of the brandy is obviously not as vital to the eventual taste as it would be if the brandy were to be drunk neat.

Brandies made to be consumed as part of a cocktail are usually blended from pot-still and column-still brandy, part (or all) of which has been matured for a short while in oak barrels. For the connoisseurs who enjoy the smoothness and elegance of a really good brandy, a pure pot-still drink, matured for a good many years, is the best. Of course, you pay a great deal more for this elegance, but this is a drink for sipping and savoring every golden mouthful.

NOTE

Some brandy lovers find that a small amount of water added to the drink helps to release the aromas. Just add a splash, no more than the brandy itself, and see for yourself whether this suits your own palate. Ice does the trick too, and is sometimes welcome on a warm evening. It also adds the satisfying tinkle of ice against glass—always a pleasant part of any drink.

To obtain the most enjoyment from your brandy, serve it in a thin-glass brandy 'balloon' designed to bring out the subtle nuances of the drink. The glass has a wide middle (as implied by the name) to allow for a large surface area, so the aromas of the spirit can be released. The glass then narrows to a small mouth, to concentrate those aromas. The short stem creates a comfortable handgrip and allows the drinker to warm the spirit slightly by cupping the balloon in the palm of the hand. The anticipation is almost as important as the swallowing.

Admire that soft golden glow, swirl the brandy gently, nose the fragrance and take a small sip. Allow it to coat the whole inside of your mouth before letting it slide down your throat.

Cognac

Cognac, rated by connoisseurs as the best brandy in the world, is made only in the Charente region of western France. Cognac is classified according to the age of the youngest brandy in the blend. For example, a * * * (three star) or V.S. Cognac must be aged for at least three years in wood before being bottled. If the bottle bears the letters VSOP it means the contents have been aged for at least four years in wood before bottling.

For the real cognac connoisseur, however, the drink to choose is Old Liqueur Cognac, also known as X.O. Extra Vieille, or Napoleon. These amber gems have been aged in wood for at least 20 years and some-times for as long as 40 years. They deserve to be sipped with great reverence.

Armagnac

Considered second only to cognac, this brandy is produced in the *département* of Gers in southeastern France. Armagnac is rather more fiery than cognac, but is still full of heady rich aromas.

Of course, it's not only France that produces fine brandies. South Africa has produced great brandies for more than a century and recent changes in liquor legislation in that country have given rise to a whole range of excellent 'boutique' brandies, produced in small quantities by wine estates. Some of the large South African brandy producers also make limited quantities of fine aged brandies.

Greece produces good brandies, too, and the Metaxa range includes some excellent brandies, increasing in age right up to their 50-year-old Grade Fine Dry.

Good brandy matures in oak barrels for at least three years before being bottled.

- ✦ Two parts old cognac
- ✦ One part tawny port
- ✦ A splash of Pernod
- ✦ A squeeze of lemon juice
- ✦ Ice

Cognac Cocktail

This is a drink that should be sipped thoughtfully, preferably in winter and beside a crackling log fire.

Place some ice in a cocktail shaker, add the cognac, port, Pernod, and lemon juice, and shake well. Strain into a lowball glass and add additional ice if required.

- ❖ One part Armagnac
- ❖ Two parts fresh lemon juice
- ❖ One teaspoon superfine sugar
- ❖ One egg white
- ❖ A dash of Angostura bitters
- ❖ Slice of orange
- ❖ Ice cubes

Armagnac Sour

If you like the idea of a sophisticated brandy cocktail, try an Armagnac Sour.

Place four cubes of ice in a cocktail shaker, add all the ingredients and shake well.
Strain into a champagne flute and garnish with a slice of orange, after squeezing a little of the juice into the drink.

- ✦ A splash of brandy
- ✦ An equal quantity of undiluted orange cordial

The Tiger

In my family it became a tradition to end the day with a 'Tiger', a drink invented by my late father. Late at night, when the coffee cups were cold and the winter fire had died to a grey ash, he would suggest, 'Shall we kill a little tiger before going upstairs to bed?'

Mix the brandy and orange cordial together. The result is a warming, sticky sweet orange liqueur that always seems exactly right for ending a good day's work.

g

grappa

UNLIKE BRANDY,
GRAPPA IS NOT BLENDED
AFTER DISTILLATION.

Grappa is a fashionable drink sometimes sold in elegant hand-blown bottles and, because of the labour involved in its production, can be very expensive. Some people like their grappa chilled and served in a martini glass. For most, however, a brandy balloon goblet is best. This allows the subtle aromas to collect at the mouth for the fullest enjoyment as just a small amount is held, tasted and savored with care. Grappa also makes a warming addition to a cup of espresso coffee. The heat of the coffee releases its aromas, creating an elegant taste experience.

"Fear the man who drinks water,
for he remembers in the morning what
the rest of us said last night."
Ancient Greek saying

The spirit of Italy

In medieval times grappa was the preserve of the landowners and their wealthy customers, but at the end of every pressing there was a chuck of compressed grape skins and pips that had to be cleared out of the wine press.

These were carefully carried home by the workers who added water to them, and left the mixture to steep and ferment until it became a rather tasteless alcoholic beverage. Later they devised ways of distilling their husk wine into a rough, but potent spirit that was the forerunner of modern grappa.

The modern version of this historic spirit starts with pomace which comprises the skins, pulp, seeds, and stems of grapes that are left behind from the making of wine. The pomace is soaked in water to extract the remaining flavor, sugars, and other compounds. This is then pressed, and the resulting juice fermented and double distilled into a spirit that is fiery and aromatic. Unlike brandy, grappa is not blended after distillation. The grape variety used in the making is the important factor and experienced grappa fans have their favourites. Grappa is not usually aged in barrels like brandy, although some upmarket brands now do an aged version. One such aged spirit is Grappa Bochino, produced in the Italian district of Friuli.

Some of the Italian grape varietals used in the better grappas include Muscat, Gavi, Cabernet Sauvignon, and Brunello. In South Africa the Dalla Cia family produces an excellent grappa from Chardonnay grapes. Good grappa is also produced in California.

When in Italy, look for good grappa brands like Jacapo Poli, Gaja, Michele Chiarlo, and Nardini.

Making a marc

In France a similar drink to grappa is made and called marc. In fact, marc is the name given to the grape pulp after it is pressed, in the same way that coffee grounds are called Marc de Café.

Marc spirit is produced in the same way as the Italian grappa and was once sold as a cheap alternative to cognac or Armignac. It was also very popular with the Impressionist painters in Paris.

One of the most elegant marcs produced today comes from the Champagne region of France and is called, appropriately, Marc de Champagne. It is considerably lighter in character than the usual, rather rough marc.

In Burgundy, a slightly different form of marc is produced from the grape residue scraped off the bottom of barrels after the clear wine has been racked off. It is known as Marc de Borgogne.

A specially distilled marc, Marc de Hospices de Beaune, is made solely for the famous annual charity auction held in Beaune. Its rarity value, and the fact that it is sold for charity, tend to make it one of the most expensive marcs available.

THE HIGH SUGAR CONTENT IN
FORTIFIED DESSERT WINES
IS A SUREFIRE REVIVER.

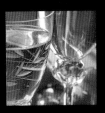

FORTIFIED WINES

The meal is over, the coffee cups are cold and the conversation is slowing down, but there's an air of quiet contentment in the room and it's obvious none of the guests is ready to go home just yet. This is a good time to offer a round of small drinks to perk up the party. Madeiras, jerepigoes, muscadels, and other fortified dessert wines are great for this. 'Fortified' wines are those where the fermentation is halted by adding brandy. This kills the unspent yeast cells leaving part of the natural sugar of the grape unfermented and giving the wine a high alcohol content. Madeira is a fortified wine considered an excellent after-dinner drink. Fortified with grape brandy, it is the only wine that improves by being heated.

"Wine whets the wit, improves its native force, and gives a pleasant flavour to discourse."
John Pomfret

Madeira

Fortification and heating were discovered accidentally. Madeira began as an export wine to the New World and during the voyage it became overheated while the barrels lay on the ships' decks under the blazing sun. Amazingly, this produced a wine with a nutty, burnt toffee flavor.

In the 18th century, winemakers discovered that adding grape brandy (fortification) resulted in an even more delicious wine. The juice ferments for two to four weeks and then grape brandy is added to kill the yeast. After the wine is 'cooked' it rests and is placed into fresh barrels. An additional hit of brandy brings the wine up to an alcohol level of about 20 per cent.

Madeira is categorized according to age. Premium Madeira usually begins with a five-year-old reserve with the primary grape variety displayed on the label. Up the scale are 10-year-old and 15-year-old reserves and 20-year-old Fresquiera. All vintage Madeiras must come from certain grape varieties, and be matured in oak casks for 20-plus years as well as two years in the bottle before being sold to the public. No wonder these precious fortified wines demand high prices.

Some of the flavors found in Madeira are reminiscent of chocolate, almonds, berries, and coffee.

Jerepigoes

Another category of fortified wine, popular among South African wine lovers, is called Jerepigo. It's certainly easier on the pocket than a Madeira.

To produce a good jerepigo the grapes (usually of the muscat grape family) are allowed to ripen until almost at the raisin stage. They are then picked and crushed and the honey-sweet juice fortified immediately with grape spirit, often before any fermentation has taken place at all. The juice is given an alcohol content of between 17 and 20 per cent by volume. (The alcohol in table wines is usually between 9 and 14 per cent by volume.) The wine is then allowed to rest, often for a year or more, to allow the juice and alcohol to 'marry' properly.

Because of their high alcohol and sugar content, good jerepigoes improve with age and can be kept for 20 years or more. A well-aged jerepigo is a real treat. This delicious drink, often described as

Its high alcohol content allows jerepigo to mature elegantly for many years.

'full-sweet', has all the original sugar still in the wine, rather than some of it converted to alcohol.

Some wine purists claim that this is not actually wine at all, in strict terms, as it has not been created by fermentation. They say it is really grape juice preserved in alcohol, but we are not here to split semantic hairs. We're here to enjoy the delights of cocktails and leave the debate to more serious minds.

Most of the good South African jerepigoes are made from the Muscat d'Alexandrie grape, known locally as 'hanepoot', which means 'cock's foot'. Some say this strange name is derived from the tendrils of the vine, which grow in the shape of a cockerel's foot. Others think it is a Dutch mistranslation of the term 'honey pot', which was used by British soldiers to describe the very sweet muscat grapes in the Cape vineyards.

Muscadels

Another member of the muscat grape family is Muscat de Frontignan, which is also used to produce fine fortified wines known in South Africa as muscadels. These come in two versions—red and

South African muscadel – pure bottled sunshine.

white—and are noted for their typical muscat honey aroma and flavor. Like all fortified wines, they make ideal after-dinner drinks, leaving the sweetest memories on the palate and providing enough alcohol to ensure a good night's sleep.

The climate in South Africa's wine-producing regions is perfect for these wines. Cool, damp winters are followed by blazing-hot summers when the grapes ripen well and develop high-sugar contents. The Cape's muscadels have been described lyrically as 'pure bottled sunshine'. Of course, South Africa is not the only country producing fine fortified dessert wines.

South Africa's sun-warmed vineyards are ideal for producing sweet, fortified wines.

Some delicious fortified wines are made in California, also using members of the Muscat grape family, usually the white Muscat de Frontignan and the black Muscat de Hamburg. They also make use of the Muscat de Alexandrie — South Africa's beloved hanepoot.

Sauternes

In quite a different category, but also comprising honey-sweet wines, are the Sauternes of France, the Noble Late Harvests of South Africa, and the Tokay wines of Hungary. These wines have a strange feature in common. They are all the result of a fungus disease called *Botrytis cinerea*, which affects some vineyards after a spell of warm, damp weather during the ripening season.

Sunshine and good, rich soil produce fine wine grapes.

The botrytis fungus coats the grapes with a nasty looking grey fuzz that creates tiny punctures in the skin of the berry. Water inside the grape escapes through these little holes, leaving the pulp highly concentrated and rich in the sugar, acid, and flavor compounds of very ripe grapes.

At this stage, the grapes are grey, wrinkled and extremely unattractive. It's a wonder that any winemaker is able to make wine from them, but with a great deal of careful pressing, cleaning and refining, a truly great wine can be created.

Because it is so labor-intensive, botrytis wine is expensive and usually sold in small bottles. However the botrytis aroma and flavor are unlike anything else in the wine range and true wine connoisseurs are willing to pay for the privilege of tasting this nectar. Small wonder the botrytis fungus has been called 'Noble Rot' in English and '*Edelfaul*' in German.

WHISKY

SCOTCH IS THE PERFECT DRINK TO SAVOR
AT THE END OF THE DAY.

Whisky has been the national drink of Scotland for more than five centuries. Whisky lovers will tell you that the word 'whisky' comes from the ancient Scottish words *uisge beatha*, or 'the water of life'. Obviously the ponderous *uisge beatha* was rather difficult to pronounce after a glass or two, so drinkers settled for the simpler 'whisky'. Only the real amber liquor of Scotland may be spelled 'whisky' (without the 'e') and only the product of Scotland may be referred to as Scotch. These are traditions fiercely guarded by lovers of this king of spirits.

In ancient times most whisky was made privately on Scottish farms. Today Scotch in all its forms—from blended whiskies to rare vatted malts—is enjoyed by connoisseurs the world over.

> "I often wonder what the vintners buy, one half so precious as the goods they sell."
>
> Omar Khayam

The history of whisky distillation

The distilling of whisky was perfectly legal in the early 1700s, as long as it was not offered for sale. Well...

Whisky production received a major boost in 1736, with the passing of the 'Gin Act' in parliament. This imposed a stiff duty on gin, but exempted aquavitae, so whisky became comparably more affordable. Later, in 1757, commercial whisky distilling was actually prohibited by the British parliament, because politicians are by nature unable to keep their busy little noses out of the affairs of honest men. It was still, however, legal for private distillers to produce whisky (but not to sell it, note) and so the owners of stills found they suddenly had a vast and eager market. Whisky smuggling became a major Scottish industry.

By 1777 there were only eight licensed distilleries left in Scotland. There were, however, more than 400 illegal stills. The Americans proved many years later with their Prohibition Act, that no amount of legislation will keep the human race away from its share of alcohol.

A question of style

I have noticed an interesting fact about whisky and those who drink it. Many people who normally drink beer or wine will suddenly order whiskies when somebody else is paying the bill.

I saw this time and time again when I was a junior manager and often had to organize company functions to entertain senior executives or important customers. People I knew socially, who invariably drank beer at home, would almost certainly order a whisky-and-soda when the waiter called for orders.

Maybe people feel that by drinking whisky they are revealing their sophisticated tastes. "We whisky-lovers are refined, and elegant," they wanted to say. "We demand the best."

There's a certain mysterious quality about whisky that makes it one of the most sought-after drinks in the world. Maybe it's the idea that great whisky comes from the remote mist-swathed highland hills of Scotland, where deep, dark peat-laden streams provide the magic ingredient that doesn't exist anywhere else.

The spirit of the Scottish highlands is captured in every bottle of great Scotch whisky.

Of course, there are whiskies and whiskies—some of them quite ordinary and inexpensive, and others rare jewels in the treasure house of drinks. And probably more nonsense is talked about whisky than any other drink on earth (except wine, of course, which is the traditional bluffer's playing-field).

Like many alcoholic drinks, whisky is quite a simple substance, made up of nothing other than water, barley and yeast.

True afficionados will tell you there is far more to it than that. Whisky, they assure us, is a concentration of the earth, water, fire, and air of Scotland. It's the very spirit of Bonnie Scotland gathered into a bottle.

Creating the magic

The first step in whisky making is to malt the barley. To do this the grain is soaked for a couple of days and then spread out on the malting floor to germinate. This malting process turns the starches in the grain into sugars.

After about a week the sprouted grain shoots will have reached their correct length and the malted barley will be transferred to kilns for drying. Traditionally, this is done over a peat fire and maltsters claim that the heady blue smoke from the peat adds to the flavor of the end product. The roots are then cleaned off and the remaining seeds ground into what is known as the grist. This is mixed with hot water (but not just any water, note. The magic, peaty streams of Scotland make the difference).

This thin porridge is diluted in a 'mash tun' and the liquid drained off. Yeast is added (the leftover husks of the mash are compressed and used as cattle feed) and the fermentation process begins. The resulting liquor, with an alcohol content of between five and 10 per cent, is finally distilled to form the basis of whisky.

Simple? Far from it. In fact the work has just begun.

This raw spirit is now matured in oak barrels for some years, tasted, blended, and cosseted by experts to produce the distinctive malt whiskeys that are respected the world over.

The whisky districts in Scotland each produce a spirit with its own unique characteristics. Whiskies from the eastern region, on the coast of Aberdeenshire, are said to be bracing and windswept in character.

Like much of the regional whisky, most of it goes into blending. Whiskies from the northern region, north of Inverness, are 'stern and muscular', as one needs to be able to survive in those extreme conditions. Glenmorangie, one of the great single malts, comes from this area. Perthshire is said to produce whiskies that are 'smooth, soft and comfortable to the palate'.

Lowland whiskies are gentle and self-effacing and often used in blends to tone down the wilder flavors of malts from other regions.

Islay malts are wild and brackish. Enthusiasts recommend Laphroaig and Ardbeg—big, heroic whiskies.

Island malts, as distinct from Islay malts, come from the islands, excluding Islay but

including the famous Oban. They vary in character, but some connoisseurs claim you can taste the tang of the northern ocean in them.

Campbelltown was once a region of more than 20 distilleries of which only Glen Scotia and Springbank remain.

Finally, there are the Speyside whiskies, produced in the area from Elgin to Dufftown. The producers claim their special magic comes from the water of the area. The whiskies are said to be pure and ethereal.

Some whisky lovers claim there's another region too— Glenlivet regarded (with considerable reverence) as belonging in a whisky world all of its own.

Island malts—a splash of warmth from the chilly northern sea.

THE POWER OF ALCOHOL WAS CLAIMED TO BE A DIVINELY INSPIRED GIFT FROM HEAVEN.

LIQUEURS

It's interesting to note how many of the world's most famous alcoholic drinks were originally—and in many cases are still—produced in monasteries. The reason for this being that the first alchemists—many of whom were monks working in monasteries distilling wines and creating pure alcohol—did so for medicinal and life-giving purposes. These early liqueurs were considered alchemical potions. It didn't take long, however, for people to realize they didn't have to be sick to enjoy them.

By the 14th century the drinking of liqueurs had become popular in Italy and had spread to France. Between the 14th and the early 17th century most of the production of these liqueurs was done by the alchemists and the monastic orders.

"Blot out every book in which wine is praised, and you blot out the world's greatest literature."

Julian Street

Elixirs of old

The early alchemists considered distilled alcohol so important that they called it the water of life—*eau de vie*. Many of the world's best known liquors, that started life as medicines, are still considered to have healing properties.

Bénédictine

The oldest liqueur in the world, Bénédictine was first made in the Benedictine Abbey of Fécamp in France in 1510 and was ostensibly designed for medicinal use.

Tradition has it that the monk, Dom Bernardo Vincelli, who discovered the formula, tasted it and remarked "Deo Optimo Maximo", which means something like, "Praise be to God, most good, most great". Since then every bottle of Bénédictine has carried the letters D.O.M.

As is often the case with liqueurs, the formula of this rare drink was once regarded as one of the world's best-kept secrets. It was produced at the monastery until the French revolution in 1789, when it was banned and the formula apparently lost.

In the 1860s, however, a descendant of one of the original monastery's lawyers rediscovered the secret formula among papers he had inherited and a private company was formed to produce the historic drink once again.

The original Bénédictine is sweet, so in the 1930s brandy was added to create a drier drink called B&B. Both Bénédictine and B&B are traditionally served straight in large liqueur glasses.

Chartreuse

Another well-known liqueur that has its roots in a religious order is Chartreuse. The original formula was created in 1605 in Grenoble, France, by the religious order of the Carthusian Fathers (Les Peres Chartreux) who gave it its name. The drink continued to be tweaked and improved until the present recipe was perfected by a member of the order in 1737.

In 1903 the order relocated to Tarragona, Spain after being expelled from its monastery under French law. The monks, however, secretly returned to France to make their precious Chartreuse. The French government looked the other way, as it had been unable to duplicate the secret formula, which was obviously a national treasure.

There are two versions of Chartreuse—yellow, which is 86 proof and green which is 110 proof. Both are plant liqueurs made from a brandy base.

PROOF

Proof is a quaint traditional British method of measuring the alcohol strength of a liquor, based on a strange system of determining how much gunpowder was needed to add to the liquor before it would ignite.

'100 Proof' spirit contains 57,1 percent alcohol. A liquor containing less alcohol than this is said to be 'under proof', while one containing more is 'over proof'. Trust the British to come up with something so ridiculously complicated.

Chartreuse is spicy and aromatic in flavor, the green liqueur being drier and more powerful than the yellow one. Recipes for the herbal liqueurs of Aiguebelle, Carmeline, La Senancole, and Trappastine were also originally monastic elixirs. Of course, as the secret recipes became less of a secret they slipped out of the hands of the monks and by the middle of the 16th century several distilleries had been formed which were producing commercial quantities of liqueurs.

Frangelico

Another popular liqueur connected with the monastic tradition is Frangelico—a delicious hazelnut-flavored drink made in Italy and exported to more than 80 countries.

The legend of Frangelico goes back more than three centuries to a monk who lived alone in a forest. Surrounded by wild hazelnuts and berries, he created the liqueur that bears his name.

Frangelico is a versatile drink that can be served with coffee, poured into it or over ice, and used as a flavoring in cocktails.

Frangelico can claim to have three centuries of tradition in every glass.

Liqueurs today

There are literally thousands of liqueurs today. They're made in almost every country of the world. All we can hope to do in a brief chapter like this is mention a few of them to whet your appetite. Let's start with an all-time favorite:

Cointreau

This aromatic drink is made from an infusion of orange peel, and other very closely guarded secret ingredients, in a base of grape brandy. It is sugar-sweet and colorless, but with a strong aroma of oranges, and some elusive herbal scents lurking under it.

It has been around since 1849, when it was created in Angers in the French Loire valley by the brothers Edouard and Adolphe Cointreau. This delicious drink is best served either on the rocks or 'frappé' (poured over finely crushed ice).

It is also one of the most versatile cocktail ingredients, as it mixes well with almost any spirit drink with the possible exception of whisky. Add it to gin and you have a White Lady. Mix it with brandy and it becomes a Sidecar. Some connoisseurs even mix it with tequila to make a lemon margarita.

Opposite: *Cointreau—the magic heart of many great cocktails.*

Another natural evening drink is a cream liqueur, and there are several from which to choose.

Bailey's Irish Cream

The makers of Bailey's Irish Cream claim that theirs is the original whiskey and cream-based liqueur and they may well be right. Because of its thick, creamy texture, it is is often served over finely crushed ice and can also be added to small cups of espresso coffee at the end of a meal, for a hot after-dinner drink. Bailey's Irish Cream is also a superb topping for an ice cream or a boozy dessert.

Cadbury's have produced a fine chocolate-cream liqueur, and a South African drink called Amarula Cream, made from the berries of a wild bushveld tree, has taken the world by storm. It was created after game viewers spotted herds of elephants swaying drunkenly in the jungle after eating the fermented berries that had fallen from the trees. And if it works for elephants, it's certainly worth a try.

Galliano

Italian Galliano is a dark-yellow liquor flavored with anise, liquorice and vanilla. It's extremely sweet, so it's often served with an equal portion of gin and a squeeze of lemon juice, resulting in a Milano.

Opposite: *Galliano's sweet and soothing flavors make it the perfect bedtime liqueur.*

Kümmel

Kümmel can lay claim to being one of the oldest liqueurs in the world and was being made in its native Holland as far back as 1500. It has a white spirit base (close to vodka) flavored with caraway seeds (and, as ever, with other secret ingredients). Kümmel is usually drunk on the rocks or over ice with a dash of lemon juice.

Glayva

Glayva is a whisky-based liqueur flavored with herbs and spices and will probably appeal to drinkers who enjoy fine Scotch whisky. Glayva is sometimes added to a glass of chilled milk, stirred well, topped with a dusting of grated nutmeg and served as a nightcap.

Glayva also makes a good hot toddy, mixed with a spoon of brown sugar, some boiling water, lemon juice and honey.

Chocolate liqueur

Chocolate liqueurs would seem to be ideal after-dinner drinks, seeing that chocolates are often passed around with the coffee after a good meal. Brand names include Cheri-Suisse, Crème de Cacao, Chocolate Suisse, and Royal Chocolate Mint Liqueur. There are many others. It would be a soothing idea to serve small glasses of chocolate liqueur instead of handing out chocolates with coffee.

Opposite: *Glayva adds a touch of Scottish warmth to a bedtime hot toddy.*

Sambucco

This Italian liqueur, made from an infusion of elder berries and licorice, is traditionally served ignited with three coffee beans floating on top. There's also a coffee-flavored version that's dark colored—almost black—called Sambucco Negra or simply Black Sambucco.

Slivovitz

Slivovitz is a Polish liquor made from dark-blue plums, double distilled and aged in oak. It can be either clear or golden in color and is a favorite drink for people of Polish ancestry.

Blue Curaçao

Blue Curaçao is an intriguing liqueur that never fails to stir the conversation because there are very few things in the normal human diet that are naturally blue. This deep-blue drink is colored with natural food dyes and is used mainly as a coloring agent for cocktails. It originated in the West Indies and is made from bitter oranges.

For a really mysterious-looking drink offer your guests a cocktail made of leftover sparkling wine;

A splash of blue adds romance to your beditme cocktail, and Curaçao supplies it.

add a splash of blue Curaçao and serve in a small cocktail glass. In spite of its unusual look, this drink is rather delicious. A slightly more complicated version, with Amaretto and lemon juice added, is known as a Ritz Fizz.

Danziger Goldwasser

A rather festive-looking liqueur for the Christmas season is the Danish drink called Danziger Goldwasser. It's a clear liqueur flavored with aniseed and caraway, with tiny flecks of gold leaf floating in it. Shake the bottle before pouring, so you get the gold twinkling gently in the glass as you drink it. There's something undeniably romantic about swallowing pure gold.

Danziger Goldwasser adds the glisten of gold to a Danish Christmas.

There's also a German version of the drink called Goldschlager and another called Bruidstranen, which means 'bride's tears'. It would be fascinating to learn the origin of the last name. Let's hope they were tears of joy.

THE NAME VODKA COMES FROM THE RUSSIAN
ZHIZNENNIA VODA, WHICH MEANS 'WATER OF LIFE'.

VODKA

Modern vodka is pure spirit distilled from any of a number of substances, including grain, sugar cane, and grapes, and then filtered through charcoal to remove certain oils and other impurities. The result is almost pure alcohol with almost no flavor or smell. In western countries vodka on its own is considered rather too fierce for most palates and it's usually used to add alcoholic fire to other drinks such as fruit juices or carbonated cool drinks. For this reason vodka is one of the world's most popular cocktail ingredients: it adds the alcohol without changing the taste. You can experiment with blends of fruit juices, mineral waters, or colas, and when you find a good flavor combination, just add vodka and voila! A new cocktail is born.

"I drink only to make my friends more interesting."
Don Marquis

The perfect mixer

Vodka blends unobtrusively with almost anything. You can even add it to clear beef bouillon to create a drink known as Bullshot. (Incidentally, doctors claim that a salty drink last thing at night helps to stave off muscle cramps, so if you're a sufferer it's worth remembering.)

In the chilly northern climates of countries like Russia, Poland and Norway, vodka is gulped straight as a sure way to warm the blood. Drinking vodka like that is not a particularly frivolous action. It tends to be serious and quick and leave some of the drinkers firmly attached to the floor. Its main task is to help the

Vodka teams up with almost any drink to prove itself the most versatile of mixers.

drinker forget the cold, and it certainly does that admirably. So unless you are made of stern stuff, or descended from people from the far northern climes, you'll probably use vodka mixed with other ingredients in a cocktail.

- ✦ A measure of vodka
- ✦ A measure of Kirsch
- ✦ A measure of Cointreau
- ✦ A measure of grapefruit juice
- ✦ Ice
- ✦ Maraschino cherry

The Salvatore

This delightful drink creates exactly the right
subtle combination of sweet and tart flavors to
end your evening with a nicely titillated palate.

Shake together all the ingredients with ice and
strain into a cocktail glass.
Add a maraschino cherry on a cocktail stick
for decoration.

- One measure vodka

- One part unsweetened grapefruit juice

- 1 teaspoon of lemon juice

- Ice

Salty Dog

The secret of this subtle little drink lies in the salt-rimmed glass. To create this, dampen the rim of a cocktail glass with lemon juice and dip it into a saucer of fine salt. Allow the glass to stand for a while so that the salt can dry into a hard crust.

Place four cubes of ice into a cocktail shaker with the vodka, grapefruit, and lemon juice. Shake the mixture well and strain it carefully into the salt-rimmed glass.

- One part fresh lime juice
- One part cherry liqueur
- Two parts vodka
- Maraschino cherry
- Crushed ice

Cherry Vodka

This pretty little drink has quite a reputation as an aphrodisiac, so serve it with caution.

Place a spoon of crushed ice in a cocktail shaker and add the lime juice, cherry liqueur and vodka.
Shake well and strain into a small cocktail glass, and decorate with a maraschino cherry.

- One part vodka

- Six parts orange juice

- Slice of banana (optional)

- Ice cubes

The Screwdriver

Vodka being clear in form lends substance to the legendary origin of the drink known as a 'Screwdriver'. Apparently construction workers used to slip a small container of vodka into their lunch pails and mix it with orange juice. If anybody asked what they had in their box they'd say: "Oh, just a screwdriver".

To make it, place several ice cubes in a cocktail shaker and add the vodka and fresh orange juice. (Use two measures of vodka if using fresh orange juice.)

Shake well and strain into a cocktail glass. Traditionally this drink is decorated by adding a slice of banana to the rim of the glass.

- The juice of one lemon
- A generous helping of good vodka
- A can of cocktail-grade tomato juice
- A sprinkling of black pepper
- A few drops of Tabasco
- A squirt of Worcestershire sauce
- Ice cubes
- Stick of celery (optional)

Bloody Mary

This is an old favorite and one of the world's best-known cocktails. Many variations are possible, with the basic ingredients being vodka and tomato juice.

Place four ice cubes in a cocktail shaker and add the lemon juice, vodka, and tomato juice. Shake well.

Trickle a few drops of Tabasco and a squirt of Worcestershire sauce into a whisky glass and swirl it round to coat the inside.

Strain the cocktail into the glass and grind a sprinkling of black pepper over it. If you have one, you can add a stick of celery as an edible stirrer.

WHEN MIXING A COCKTAIL NIGHTCAP, GO FOR ONE
THAT'S SMALL AND POWERFUL.

LNC

late-night
cocktails

Cocktails are fun to drink. Although they are usually served at the beginning of the evening, to break the ice, as it were, and get conversation flowing, there's no reason why they shouldn't be the last soothing drink of the day too.

No-one knows for certain where the word 'cocktail' originated. Some say it was derived from a drink called 'Coquetel' served to French officers in the southern States of the USA during the American War of Independence (1775–1783).

Others say the cocktail was the product of the American Prohibition era in the 1920s. However, as cocktails have been dated as far back as 1806, it could be that Prohibition merely popularized them, with owners of 'speakeasies' disguising the appearance of alcoholic drinks to stay one jump ahead of the police.

"There can't be good living where there is not good drinking."
Benjamin Franklin

A delectable mix

For some reason, cocktails based on brandy or whisky seem to be more appropriate than those based on gin or vodka for a late-night drink, although I have included my version of a Bloody Mary in the list.

The following are all well-known cocktail names, but they've been altered slightly to turn them into late-night drinks. Cocktail purists might shudder at the sacrilege of tampering with the classics, but we all find our own favorites.

Classic cocktails, like classic cars, are timeless in their appeal.

Obvious choices for late-night cocktails include drinks like the strangely named Bull's Milk (*see* p116). A slightly modified Bull's Milk could be made by putting a measure of good brandy into a cocktail shaker with three ice cubes. Add a half-cup of full-cream milk and a teaspoon of honey and shake well. Strain into a cocktail glass and sprinkle a dusting of cinnamon over it before drinking.

Other natural choices of late-night cocktails are The Banshee (*see* p118), and Brandy Manhattan (*see* p121). Quite a good way to signal the end of an evening is for the host to suggest a bedtime cocktail. The message, "Is anybody in the mood for a final cocktail?" should give the hint that it's almost closing time. A good thing about this is that you can mix a batch of cocktails at once, and pour it into small glasses.

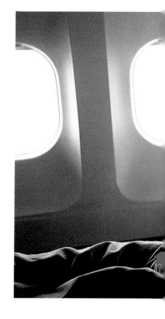

I find it extremely hard to fall asleep on an airliner. I'm sure it must be easier up in the first and business-class sections of the aircraft, but I invariably travel cattle class, squeezed between an obese woman and a huge Texan who snores. Sleep does not come easily, but a nightcap often helps.

The right bedtime cocktail ensures a peaceful night's sleep,
wherever you are.

Over the years I have found that a well-made cocktail is the perfect night-time drink in the air. Some airlines do cocktails well, others are completely hopeless. I am often tempted to select my airline according to the quality of their cocktails. Well, it's as good a criterion as any.

- One part brandy
- One cup of milk
- Sugar syrup
- Grated nutmeg
- Finely ground cinnamon
- Ice cubes

Bull's Milk

With the bull being a symbol of bravery and awesome power, this cocktail is one that no macho male should quibble with.

Place four or five ice cubes in a cocktail shaker and add the brandy, milk, and sugar syrup to taste. Shake the mixture well and then strain it into a highball glass.

Sprinkle the nutmeg and cinnamon over it and serve immediately.

- One part banana-cream liqueur
- One part chocolate liqueur or Crème de Cacao
- A dash of sugar syrup
- A slice of kiwi fruit or fresh peach
- Ice

The Banshee

Hot chocolate is a traditional bedtime drink, so why not substitute it with a cold chocolate drink. Here's a wicked one.

Pour the chocolate liqueur into a shaker with ice and add an equal part of banana-cream liqueur and a dash of sugar syrup. Shake well and strain into a cocktail glass and decorate with a slice of kiwi fruit if available. A slice of fresh peach works well here too.

+ A few drops of Angostura bitters

+ Four parts brandy

+ One part sweet Vermouth

+ Maraschino cherry (plus cocktail stick)

+ Ice cubes

Brandy Manhattan

Many people enjoy a glass of brandy before retiring to bed. You could add a new dimension to your brandy by making it part of a cocktail, as in this drink.

Place four ice cubes in a tall glass and splash a few drops of Angostura bitters over them. Add the brandy and the sweet Vermouth and stir well. Strain into a cocktail glass and decorate with a maraschino cherry on a cocktail stick.

WARM THOUGHTS

WT

A HOT TODDY AT
BEDTIME IS THE
PERFECT WAY
TO KEEP WINTER
CHILLS AT BAY.

Sometimes a chilly winter night calls for a hot drink before retiring to bed. Now cocoa may be perfect for the children or granny, but in cooler countries there's a strong tradition of serving hot alcoholic drinks to keep out the winter chills.

Whether you decide on a hot toddy, an Irish coffee, a glogg or a glühwein, a warming drink at bedtime will guarantee a good night's sleep.

Most of these warm drinks are traditionally made in large quantities, rather than one glass at a time. This is because it's rather a fiddly business heating up a single cup of wine, brandy, and spices, stirring it and then straining off the unwanted solids. It is far easier to make a good generous potful and share it with friends.

"Only Irish coffee provides, in a single glass, all four essential food groups: alcohol, caffeine, sugar, and fat."
Alex Levine

Hot toddy

The word 'toddy' has several interesting origins, all of them relating to drinks in some way. In India, a toddy was a spirit distilled from fermented palm sap. In Southeast Asia a toddy is a drink made from fermented coconut milk.

The original English toddy was simply a small measure, or nip. A 'hot toddy' was any of a number of hot drinks, usually served at bedtime to ward off colds. A typical hot toddy could be made by adding sugar to a generous measure of brandy, topping it up with hot water and serving it with a twist of lemon and a dusting of ground cinnamon. Honey could be used instead of the sugar. A Scottish 'hot brick toddy' is a similar drink, but obviously makes use of whisky instead of brandy, and the addition of a small pat of butter.

Mulled wine or ale

In 17th century England it was a popular practice to mull wine or ale in winter. This was done by adding spices, lemon and sometimes a beaten egg to the drink, in a lidded silver jug, then heating it by plunging in a red-hot poker. It was never heated over a stove or allowed to boil, as this would have caused some of the alcohol to evaporate.

Not many homes have open fires anymore, so red-hot pokers are probably rather rare. Electric stove plates, however, can be used to good effect to warm the drink without letting it boil.

Following is a selection of hot bedtime drinks from around the world. Use these recipes as a basis to create your own versions.

- ✦ A bottle of red wine
- ✦ A bottle of medium sherry
- ✦ Half a cup of sugar
- ✦ Half a bottle of brandy
- ✦ Eight dashes of Angostura bitters
- ✦ A handful of raisins
- ✦ A few unsalted almonds

Glogg

Drinkers should be aware of the high alcohol content of this Scandinavian punch. It's obviously a drink suitable for glugging immediately before falling into bed.

Heat the mixture in a large saucepan, stir well and then pour into mugs containing raisins and unsalted almonds.

- ✦ A bottle of red wine
- ✦ A dash of brandy
- ✦ The juice and zest of two lemons
- ✦ Half a cup of hot water
- ✦ Half a cup of brown treacle sugar
- ✦ A teaspoon of whole cloves
- ✦ One stick of cinnamon
- ✦ A sprinkling of powdered ginger

Glühwein

Make this traditional German drink by placing the lemon juice, zest, hot water, sugar, cloves, cinnamon, and powdered ginger in a saucepan.

Warm the mixture to almost boiling point, stirring occasionally, then add the red wine and bring it up to almost boiling temperature again. A dash of brandy adds an extra zip.

Strain the mixture into mugs and serve.

- ✦ A cup of very strong coffee
- ✦ Two teaspoons of sugar
- ✦ A generous dollop of Irish whiskey
- ✦ Three tablespoons of heavy cream

Irish Coffee

This is an old favorite that's enjoyed in almost every country.

A good Irish coffee is usually served in a tall glass mug. To make one, pour a cup of very strong coffee into the mug, add the sugar and Irish whiskey and stir.

Now take some thick cream and pour it gently on top of the coffee mixture, taking care to keep the two colours separated. The best way to do this is to pour the cream over the back of a teaspoon so it spreads easily on to the coffee's surface without mixing.

+ A glass of hot milk

+ A generous splash of Jamaica Rum

+ A measure of coffee liqueur

+ Cinnamon stick

Hot Jamaica Cow

Jamaicans often give milk drinks a kick by adding alcohol.

Pour a glass of hot milk into a warmed mug.

Add a generous splash of Jamaica Rum and a measure of coffee liqueur.

Stir with a cinnamon stick and serve.

+ **A good measure of Scotch whisky**

+ **Sugar to taste**

+ **A few cloves**

+ **Hot water (as desired)**

Hot Bush

Nothing to do with American presidents,
this drink is considered by many Scots
to be the perfect nightcap.

Enjoy this good measure of Scotch whisky, flavored with sugar
to taste. Add a few cloves to the mixture and top up with hot water
as you desire.

- ◆ A good measure of Kahlúa
- ◆ Hot, ready-made Horlicks
- ◆ Two tablespoons of cream
- ◆ A few chocolate vermicelli

Kahlúa Horlicks

This is one of our own favorite bedtime drinks, dreamed up by a Cape Town restaurateur. Its international character comes from the fact that Horlicks is an English malt-flavored milk drink and Kahlúa is a coffee-flavored Mexican liqueur.

To make this drink, pour a good measure of Kahlúa into a tall coffee mug and fill it with hot, ready-made Horlicks, stirring it well into a froth. Float a thin layer of cream on top of the Horlicks and sprinkle a few chocolate vermicelli on the surface before serving.

THE AGE-OLD QUESTION REMAINS: 'IS THERE REALLY SUCH A THING AS AN EFFECTIVE APHRODISIAC?'

LP
LOVE
POTIONS

It's probably because of our inherent laziness that we have believed throughout the ages in the existence of magic potions. How much simpler life would be if we could slip a drop of magic potion into our loved-one's cup to have her fall madly in love with us. The search continues, but tradition tells us that at the slightest miscalculation you'll have your friends turning into enemies and your loved ones falling for a donkey, as happened in Shakespeare's Midsummer Night's Dream.

We should never forget that the most powerful erogenous zone on the human body is the brain; it constantly absorbs all kinds of stimuli. If you're looking for a love potion, consider the messages you want conveyed to your beloved's mind. The rest is merely smoke and mirrors.

"Drink has caused many a lady to be loved who otherwise might have died single."
Finley Peter Dunne

Awakening the senses

Most animals rely almost entirely on scent to attract sexual partners. When a female is ready for sex, she emits a pheromone that tells the male she's ready for love. Fruit farmers use synthesized pheromones to attract insects to their traps. The poor little females come homing in on an irresistible perfume, only to find themselves stuck to a sheet of glue. (Maybe you've had similar experiences on a blind date, yes?)

The power of scent as a sex attractant is rather less developed in humans, but it's certainly there. The perfume industry earns billions of dollars annually selling scents their customers believe will make them more attractive to other humans. So when mixing your love potion, make sure it has an attractive aroma.

Italian-born winemaker Giorgio Dalla Cia says he believes Pinot Noir wine contains a high pheromone component. "It has the scent of truffles," he says, "and the reason truffles are so sought-after is that they are great aphrodisiacs."

Chocolate delight

Chocolate is said to be a mild sexual stimulant, and so are roses. Do you think it's mere coincidence that love-sick swains tend to present their partners with bunches of roses or boxes of chocolates? Colors, too have become associated with symbols of love. They feature in the red hearts on a Valentine's Day card, for example, in pink roses or in the white of a bridal gown.

The tactile experience

Physical love is a very tactile activity, so texture plays an important role in your love potion's recipe. Think of something smooth and creamy.

This suggests a chocolate liqueur (*see* Chocolate Cocktail; p144) as a good starting point, possibly topped with a layer of sweet, heavy cream. Now we're getting somewhere.

The power of association

Memory is quite a powerful ingredient of any love potion. If you once spent a romantic time on the Greek island of Santorini years ago, sipping retsina in the moonlight before making wonderful love, chances

The right drink can trigger deliciously romantic memories.

are that recreating that scene by serving chilled retsina to a background recording of bouzouki music may, in itself, prove to be a highly effective aphrodisiac.

Remember the evening you both drank those delicious Bloody Marys by the pool and then made wonderful love on the grass in the sunset? All you have to do is mix up a Bloody Mary (see p109) and suggest that, as it's a warm evening, you should sip it at the poolside. You can't go wrong.

One essential ingredient in the love potion armory should be the aptly named Parfait Amour. This French liqueur has a seductive lilac color and is flavored with rose petals, vanilla, and almonds, all of which contribute to its reputation as a love potion.

Champagne is often associated with romantic occasions, so no list of love potions would be complete without at least one champagne-based cocktail.

All the drinks mentioned here are just a part of the recipe for romance. The remaining ingredients are woven round the love potions in the form of the right place, the romantic surroundings, the soft sounds, and sensual scents. The most carefully prepared drink in the world will count for nothing if it is served in haste and plonked down unceremoniously in an unattractive glass. Love potions must be stirred with passion and served with gentle care. No matter how 'modern' we like to think we are, a touch of old-fashioned romanticism never goes amiss. A single rose on the serving tray between two elegant cocktail glasses sends an irresistible message.

- ✦ A heaped teaspoon of cocoa
- ✦ A generous splash of ruby port
- ✦ A generous measure of Galliano
- ✦ One egg yolk
- ✦ Ice cubes

Chocolate Cocktail

**Let's try a traditional Chocolate Cocktail
as a start to a romantic night.**

Place the powdered chocolate in a cocktail shaker
with four ice cubes.

Add the ruby port and the Galliano, then drop in the
yolk of an egg.

Shake well until it attains a silky texture.

Strain into two cocktail glasses, sit close together
and sip the potion slowly.

- One part vodka
- One part peach schnapps or peach brandy
- Six parts of fresh orange juice
- Twist of orange zest
- Ice cubes

Fuzzy Navel

The Fuzzy Navel is rather a charming little drink.

To make it, pour the vodka, peach schnapps or peach brandy and the orange juice into a cocktail shaker with some ice cubes.

Shake well and strain into glasses, decorating each one with a twist of orange zest.

The 'parts' mentioned here could be a regular spirit measure (sometimes called a 'jigger', or a 'tot') for one or two people, all the way up to full cups for a party of six or more.

- A measure of cherry liqueur
- One part Parfait Amour
- Two tablespoons of sweet cream

Love Bite

For a friendly end to a romantic evening, a Love Bite is the perfect shared nightcap. It requires a steady hand to make. Pour two and hand one to your partner.

Take two shot glasses and pour the cherry liqueur into the bottom of each. Carefully trickle the Parfait Amour on to it, taking care not to let the two mix too much.

Float a layer of sweet cream on top.

Eye contact.

Aye,

Contact!

- ✦ Ice cubes
- ✦ Equal parts of

  Brandy

  White rum

  Cointreau
- ✦ Juice of half a lemon
- ✦ Twist of lemon rind

Between the Sheets

To make this excellent soporific, place several ice cubes in a cocktail shaker and add the brandy, white rum, and Cointreau, as well as the lemon juice. Shake the mixture well and strain into a cocktail glass, garnishing it with the lemon rind.

boozy desserts

bd

YOU DON'T NECESSARILY HAVE
TO WAIT UNTIL THE MEAL IS
OVER BEFORE ENJOYING THAT
LAST LIQUEUR OR SPIRIT.

Of course, it's perfectly acceptable to mix alcohol and dessert for a tasty end to a good meal. Almost any sweet liqueur can be poured over a scoop of vanilla ice cream to turn a boring, unimaginative dish into an exotic treat. To make it even more spectacular, soak fresh peach slices in brandy for a day before the party, and place one on top of each helping of fortified ice cream just before it is served.

Trifle is probably one of the best-known English-style desserts. Glacé cherries, walnuts, strawberry jelly, and many other additions can be included to add new dimension to your trifle. As long as there's plenty of sherry in it, you can be sure your guests will love it.

"Candy is dandy but liquor is quicker."
Ogden Nash

Fast and easy recipes

Exciting homemade boozy desserts can take just moments to prepare. See what's in your cupboard and use your imagination.

Ready-made chocolate sauce can be used as a fast topping. Buy a bottle from your local supermarket and keep it handy. It lasts for ages. Try placing squares of pound cake (leftovers from tea, maybe?) in individual bowls, soaking them in Galliano liqueur and topping them with instant chocolate. There's a winner!

Interesting jellies can be created by replacing half the water called for in their preparation, with peppermint liqueur or cherry brandy, before allowing them to set.

Explore the world of spirits and liqueurs for new tastes and keep them in mind as flavor enhancers. You can turn any traditional dessert into a memorable taste adventure. A splash of alcohol adds zest to almost any dessert. A good idea is to buy fresh soft fruit like peaches, apricots, plums, or pears when they are in season. Peel them, remove the pips, pack them carefully in glass jars and cover them with brandy, or an appropriate liqueur, before sealing them. You may need to top up the liquor from time to time as the fruit absorbs the alcohol.

When you need an instant dessert, all you need do is place a couple of pieces of the boozy fruit in small bowls and top them with whipped cream. The remaining fruit-flavored liquor can be kept as an exciting ingredient for a cocktail at a later stage.

Following are some old favourites given an added lift by the addition of a little wine or spirit.

- ✦ A large slab of dark, bitter chocolate
- ✦ A small slab of creamy milk chocolate
- ✦ Eight fresh eggs, separated
- ✦ One bar measure of brandy
- ✦ Half a bar measure of Van Der Hum liqueur or Cointreau
- ✦ Sugar to taste
- ✦ Lemon zest

Chocolate Mousse

Melt the chocolate slabs together in a double boiler, taking care not to allow any water to splash into the chocolate, as this ruins the texture. Stir until it is an even dark color. Set aside.

Separate the eggs, then whip the egg whites until very stiff. Add the brandy and liqueur to the slightly cooled chocolate mixture and fold it into the whites.

Pour the chocolate mixture over the stiff egg whites, fold together until you have a frothy texture. Spoon the mixture into glasses of your choice, then set aside to chill overnight.

Garnish with lemon zest prior to serving.

- ✦ Four oranges

- ✦ One pineapple

- ✦ Other fruit as available, especially melon

- ✦ A bar measure of cherry brandy

- ✦ Half a cup of sweet, fortified wine

- ✦ Juice of half a lemon

- ✦ A teaspoon of finely chopped mint

- ✦ Sugar

Fruit Salad

A little alcohol even perks up the old favorite.

This is about as simple as a recipe can get.
Just chop the fruit into a bowl, sprinkle sugar to taste
and add the booze and mint.
Stir gently and stand in the fridge for several hours
to allow the alcohol to flavor the fruit.

- ✦ Three tablespoons of honey
- ✦ Half a cup of Cointreau
- ✦ A mixture of about 10 glacé cherries and five walnuts finely chopped together.

Hot Honey Sauce

The popular dessert—ice cream and a hot sauce—is given a new look with this rather delicious and alcoholic sauce used instead of boring old chocolate.

Place all the ingredients in a double boiler and heat until the sauce is thin and easily poured, stirring all the time.
Take care not to heat it for too long or the alcohol will evaporate.
When ready, pour it over individual scoops of vanilla ice cream.

- ✦ One small slab of chocolate
- ✦ One cup of white sugar
- ✦ Three tablespoons of unsalted butter
- ✦ One cup of fresh cream
- ✦ A half a cup of medium
  cream sherry
- ✦ One teaspoon of vanilla essence

Hot Chocolate Sauce

If you prefer a more traditional chocolate sauce, you can give it a lift by adding a half a cup of medium cream sherry to the chocolate mixture. Here's another really decadent recipe.

Melt the chocolate in a saucepan.

Mix the sugar, butter, and cream with the melted chocolate and stir until the sugar is dissolved.

Heat for about five minutes without stirring, then add the sherry and vanilla.

Set the pot over hot water to keep the sauce warm until you are ready to serve it.

✦ Two cups of medium cream sherry

✦ Yolks of two eggs (beaten slightly)

Sherry Sauce

Desserts need not be elaborate affairs needing a great deal of work. Sometimes the simplest ones are the best. A simple sherry sauce will turn leftover pound cake or any steamed dessert into a gourmet dessert.

Warm the medium cream sherry in a double boiler.
Add the egg yolks to the sherry (still in the double boiler) and whisk the mixture until it is thick and frothy.
Pour over the cake or steamed dessert.
Serve immediately.

✦ Two large, ripe peeled bananas

✦ One cup of milk

✦ One large tablespoon of honey

✦ Two cups of soft ice cream

✦ Half a cup of medium

   cream sherry

✦ A pinch of nutmeg

✦ A pinch of salt

Sherry Shake

The last recipe in this list could be termed either
a dessert or a nightcap drink, depending on how hard
or soft your ice cream is.

In a blender, place all the ingredients together.
Blend until smooth and foamy and serve in wine glasses.
Provide thick straws if the shake is liquid, or teaspoons
if it's too thick to sip.

A CIGAR, SMOKED IN PEACE, FILLS THE AIR
WITH A SPICY RICHNESS.

lighting up

A good cigar is more than just a roll of pungent tobacco leaves. Its enjoyment at the end of a good meal is a symbol of the good life.

Unfortunately, this is not the first era in which anti-smoking sentiments have been widespread. Smoking was regarded with anger by many of the world's rulers in the 1600s. Pope Urban VIII issued a papal bill in which he banned the use of tobacco in any form in or near churches. Anybody found using tobacco would be excommunicated, he decreed.

Murad IV, a Turkish sultan, proclaimed that anybody found smoking should have their ears and noses chopped off. By 1800, however, tobacco won the battle and one by one, the governments of the world conceded victory.

"Perfection is such a nuisance that I often regret having cured myself of using tobacco."
Emile Zola

Up in smoke

France created a tobacco monopoly in 1811. The British Parliament passed a law governing the tobacco production in 1821. Cigar factories sprung up, first in Seville in Spain, then in France, Germany, and Britain. In an historic move, King Ferdinand of Spain proclaimed the Spanish colony of Cuba as a free tobacco-growing and marketing area. The rest, as they say, is history and Cuba is now recognized as the origin of the world's most sought-after cigars.

By 1840 13-million cigars were imported into Britain annually. They were expensive, and smoking them was considered a sign of wealth. They are still expensive and still regarded as a sign of good living.

Cigar know-how

In Rudman's *Complete Pocket Guide to Cigars*, the late Theo Rudman explains the make-up and manufacture of a good cigar. "The construction of a cigar is crucial to its smoking enjoyment. If it is under-filled it will draw easily, but burn too fast and get hot and harsh as a result. If it is over-filled it will have drawing difficulties or be 'plugged'. Plugging can also arise if the inner leaves are not folded correctly."

An interesting feature he describes is the fermentation of tobacco leaves for cigar production. Cigar tobacco is fermented several times by stacking it in hot, humid conditions and turning the stacks (called burros) regularly.

Some leaves are up to three years old before being considered ready for use. This fermentation process removes nicotine, tar, ammonia and other impurities from the tobacco, making it more palatable and less harmful to the lungs than normal cigarette tobacco.

Theo Rudman suggests that the beginner cigar smoker should start by trying the smaller cigars from Holland or Denmark. These include brand names like Ritmeester, Villiger, Schimmelpenninck, and Christian of Denmark.

"Before reaching the goal of Havanas," he writes, "it would be a good idea to progress to the small cigars of the Honduras and Nicaragua, as these are closer in body to cigars from Cuba than those from any other country."

Rules of etiquette

As with so many facets of the good life, cigar smoking has its little rules of etiquette and their correct observance will raise a nod of approval from the affi-cionados. Knowing the social rules is, after all, what separates the gentlemen from the yobbos.

The rich aroma of a good cigar sends out a message of good living.

Cigars should never be smoked during a meal. Their rich aroma can interfere with the enjoyment of the subtle tastes of food and ruin the occasion for others. Smoking a good cigar should never be hurried. "A Corona will probably take about 30 minutes to smoke," says Rudman, "whereas a Robusto or Churchill will demand 45 minutes. The larger sizes are much more appropriate for relaxed, late-night smoking." As an aside, he mentions that it is considered bad form in Japan for a guest or businessman to smoke a cigar larger than that of his host or superior.

When smoking in private, even in the privacy of your own home, confine your smoking to the living room and never smoke in bedrooms because, as attractive as the aroma of fresh cigar smoke might be, the smell of stale tobacco smoke is offensive and can linger for several days.

If you offer a cigar to a guest in your own home it is not

A designated smoking area is a must, even in your own home.

considered good manners to hand him a single cigar. The correct form is to offer the box, or humidor, and allow him to select the one he wants. "To offer cigars to a cigar smoker," Rudman says, "is a symbol of friendship and respect."

The sharing of a peaceful moment after dinner, quietly puffing on a good cigar, is undoubtedly an act of companionship.

Cigar sizes

Cigars come in a wide range of sizes, each with its traditional name, depending on length and diameter. The biggest available is the Double Corona, which is an impressive 7¾in (194mm) long. Other sizes include:

Demi-Tasse — 4in (100mm)

Cigarillos — 4¼in (102mm)

Half Corona — 4¼in (102mm)

Robusto/Rothschild — 4¾in (124mm)

Belvederas — 5in (125mm)

Petit Corona — 5in (129mm)

Corona — 5½in (142mm)

Panatela — 6in (154mm)

Corona Grandes — 6½in (162mm)

Slim Panatela — 6¾in (170mm)

Churchill — 7in (178mm)

Thicknesses are not listed here, but the thickness of a cigar makes a big difference to the coolness of the smoke. The thicker the cigar the cooler the smoke. For those who take small puffs, however, a thin cigar will provide a mouthful of smoke with less effort. A good cigar, a glass of fine brandy or Scotch and time to enjoy them in relaxed company could all add up to the perfect end to a memorable meal.

THE PERFECT AFTER-DINNER DRINK
SHOULD BE SERVED IN AN ATMOSPHERE
OF TRANQUIL CONTENTMENT

bedtime tales
BT

The meal was good, the company was stimulating and the conversation inspiring. Now it's time to unwind, prod a few last flickering flames from the dying embers of the fire, and of the day.

The drink that's appropriate now is a short one, but one that's full of concentrated flavor, meant to be sipped very slowly so each precious drop is savored to the full. This is why liqueurs are so often served with coffee. They fit the bill exactly.

Ideally the drink should have a story to go with it. What follow are some of my own favorite after-dinner drinks with the stories that accompany them. No-one is ever too old for a bedtime story.

"Oh God of Wine, deliver me now

half across life's stormy sea from snares

and sins of every sort,

and bring me safely back to Port."

anon

Southern Comfort

This is a delicious whiskey-based drink flavored with peaches and oranges, made in the USA with a hefty 50 per cent alcohol content.

I developed my love for this liqueur on a yacht voyage from Cape Town to St Helena in the days before GPS position finders, when navigation was still a matter of taking working out one's position with the help of a sextant and nautical tables.

The trouble with that old system is that one does need to see the sun—or stars—to be able to navigate. For five days we had sailed in thick cloud and fog conditions and all we could do, my fellow navigator, George, and I, was make a calculated guess, or 'dead reckoning' as to where we were.

After five days of guesswork, the little dot we made on the chart could have been 100 miles off-course. The others on board had no idea how unsure we two were of our position and kept asking: "When will we arrive? Should we start unpacking our shore clothes?"

We could only tell them that if our calculations were correct, we should see the island sometime the following day. Clean clothes came out, beards were shaved, hair trimmed, as George and I anxiously scanned the misty horizon for any sight of land. For all we knew, we could have passed the island two days before.

Then suddenly, exactly as our guesstimates had predicted, the clouds opened up, a shaft of brilliant sunlight hit the sea ahead of us and there was the island, not two miles away, dead ahead. Two dolphins leaped out of the water across our bows. Nobody else understood our utter relief. Only the two of us knew how lucky we had been. We went below, cracked open a bottle of Southern Comfort, poured two very large glasses and toasted our unbelievable good fortune. Today, whenever I am lucky, I feel like repeating that toast.

Calvados

This powerful spirit drink distilled from apples always reminds me of an epic scooter journey through Europe with a friend.

We were sharing a little Vespa scooter and had been travelling for some four weeks when we reached Normandy, home of apple cider and Calvados. The scooter was seriously overloaded. There is not much luggage space on such a tiny vehicle at the best of times, let alone on a 6000km journey.

We stopped at a distillery that advertised fine Calvados for tasting. The Calvados was seriously delicious. We also tasted Pommeau— an interesting drink made of apple cider fortified with Calvados— which was equally tempting. My friend decreed that we should buy a bottle of each to take with us. As the driver, I protested that there was not enough space on board for another two bottles of anything. We were dangerously overloaded already. She was insistent, however, and marched out to the scooter, extracted an expensive pair of Italian shoes from her bag and tossed them under a nearby hedge. They were replaced by the two precious bottles.

In retrospect, I've often considered it to have been a wise exchange. After all, you can buy Italian shoes almost anywhere in the world.

Grappa

Grappa—known as 'Marc' in France (see p64)—is the brandy distilled from the pressed grape skins left over after winemaking.

Originally this was a drink made by the peasant farm laborers who could not afford real brandy, but it has become refined and sought-after as an elegant digestif.

Some years ago I was involved in a film project in the winelands of the Cape and part of the programme was to shoot a film about the Meerlust Estate and its winemaker, Italian-born Giorgio Dalla Cia.

The camera rolled and I arrived in the spacious farm kitchen, where Giorgio seated me and offered me a warming cup of espresso coffee, liberally laced with his own grappa ("in the Italian style," he explained). We sipped and chatted.

Then the cameraman decided he would like the same scene shot from the other side,

Italian-born winemaker, Giorgio dalla Cia is one of the few Grappa distillers in the Cape.

A splash of grappa in your espresso coffee makes a welcome winter drink.

so I arrived in the kitchen again, was seated and offered another cup of espresso generously laced with grappa.

We sipped and chatted.

They then wanted a third shot, this time from behind, with the huge fireplace in the background. I arrived a third time, sat down and was offered espresso generously laced with grappa. We sipped again. By the time the scene was shot to the director's satisfaction, several takes later, I was in no state to continue filming and spent the rest of the morning sleeping soundly under a shady oak tree. I was informed rather rudely at lunch time that grappa made me snore.

If there are ever other drinking films in my future, I shall insist on the bottles being filled with water. I must confess, though, that real grappa and strong espresso coffee make a very warming drink to end a day. Certainly very soporific.

Dutch Gin, or Jenever

One freezing, drizzly night I stepped off the cross-channel ferry in Hoek van Holland on my way to Rotterdam.

It was about midnight and I was exhausted. The town seemed almost deserted but I spotted a light streaming from the door of a small hotel bar and went in to look for a room for the remainder of the night. Three old Dutchmen were at the bar drinking glasses of a very traditional Dutch grain gin called Jonge Bols. They invited me to join them, and offered a drink to help keep out the cold.

After they'd bought a round, I naturally returned the compliment and we settled down to some serious cementing of international ties.

Two interesting things happened. For one, I discovered I was no longer tired. In fact, we kept up our drinking until sunrise, and I then no longer felt the need for a bed. It was too late, anyway. The other interesting thing was that I was, by now, speaking very fluent Dutch. In fact, my drinking companions remarked on my accent and decided I must hail from somewhere near the Belgian border. Amazing! A whole new vocabulary in a bottle!

Re-reading the above I cannot honestly recommend Dutch Gin as a nightcap, unless you're not planning to sleep.

A wise South African winemaker, Abrie Bruwer of Springfield Estate, starts each vintage by handing out sugar-coated doughnuts to all the labourers on the farm. He believes that when you have sweetness in your mouth you will find sweetness in your heart.

"Nobody can work well with a heart full of anger or bitterness," he says. "Vines that are planted with joy, and grapes that are picked in happiness, are sure to produce wines that can be sipped with pleasure."

The wines he produces certainly seem to prove his theory.

When the pressure in his winery becomes too frantic at harvest time, and tempers become frayed, Abrie has been known to stop everything, gather his workers around him, tell them

epilogue

to relax and smile, and send them home to cool down. "It's no use working while you're angry," he says.

"Perhaps we can carry this idea one step further and make it a rule to end each day with sweetness as a step to sweet dreams. And it's not only the sweetness on the tongue that counts. Let's close the day with sweet music, sweet friendship, sweet thoughts, and sweet wine."

GLOSSARY

Akvavit — A grain or potato-based spirit from the Scandinavian countries, flavored with aromatic seeds and spices, especially caraway. Also known as aquavit.

Amontillado — A pale medium-dry Spanish sherry.

Angostura bitters — *Trademark*. A bitter aromatic tonic, used as a flavoring in alcoholic drinks.

Armagnac — Dry brandy distilled in the Gers district of France, formerly known as Armagnac.

Benedictine — A greenish-yellow liqueur made from a secret formula developed at the Benedictine monastery at Fécamp in France in about 1510.

Bordeaux — A red or white wine produced in the region around Bordeaux, France.

Botrytis cinerea — A fungus disease also known as 'Noble Rot' in English and *Edelfaul* in German. The fungus coats the grapes with a grey fuzz that creates punctures in their skins.

Brandy — An alcoholic liquor distilled from wine or fermented grape juice.

Cabernet Sauvignon — A dry, red wine made from a black grape variety originating in Bordeaux. Also found in Napa (USA), South Africa and Australia.

Champagne — A bottle-fermented sparkling white wine made from a blend of grapes, especially chardonnay and pinot noir, produced in the Champagne region of France.

Chardonnay — A dry, white table wine made from a grape variety also used to make champagne and white Burgundy.

Chartreuse — A trademark used for a usually yellow or green liqueur made from herbs and flowers.

Chianti — A dry, red table wine made from a blend of different varieties of grapes, originally produced in northwest Italy.

Cognac — A brandy distilled from white wine and produced in the French Cognac area.

Cointreau — An orange-flavored French liqueur that is a colorless form of curaçao, created in 1849 in France by confectioner Adolphe Cointreau and his brother, Edouard-Jean.

Digestif — Alcohol drunk after a meal to promote or aid digestion.

Dom Pedro - South African "adult milkshake" made by mixing ice cream with whisky.

Gewürztraminer — A white table wine with a spicy bouquet, made from this grape and produced in the Alsace region of France.

Glogg — A hot punch made of red wine, brandy, and sherry, flavored with almonds, raisins, and orange peel.

Glühwein — Red wine with sugar and spices, usually served heated.

Galliano — Golden Italian liqueur flavored with anise, liquorice and vanilla.

Jamaica rum — A highly flavored rum produced in Jamaica.

Kahlúa — Coffee-flavored liqueur made in Mexico.

Kirsch — A colorless brandy made from the fermented juice of cherries.

Kümmel — A colorless liqueur flavored chiefly with caraway seeds.

Madeira — A fortified dessert wine, from the island of Madeira.

Marc — Brandy distilled from grape or apple residue.

Muscadel — A family of related grape varieties usually used to produce rich, sweet wines, made in Italy, Spain, France, and South Africa.

Oloroso — A full-bodied, medium-sweet sherry.

Parfait Amour — French liqueur with a seductive lilac color, flavored with rose petals, vanilla, and almonds.

Pernod — Anise and licorice-flavored liqueur.

Pinot noir — 1. Red wine grape; grown especially in Burgundy, France. Now cultivated worldwide.

2. An earthy red table wine made from purple Pinot noir grapes.

Pomace — The pulp remaining after the juice has been pressed from fruit such as apples or grapes.

Port — A rich, usually sweet, fortified wine, from the Duoro Valley in Portugal.

Retsina — A Greek white or rosé wine flavored with pine resin.

Rosé — Any pink wine, made either by removing the skins of red grapes after only a little color has been extracted or by mixing red and white wines.

Rum — An alcoholic liquor distilled from fermented molasses or sugar cane.

Sambuca — An Italian liqueur made from elderberries and flavored with licorice.

Sauternes — A delicate sweet white wine from the southern Bordeaux region of France, made from grapes that have been infected with Noble Rot (see Botrytis cinerea).

Schnapps — Any of various strong, dry distilled liquors.

Sherry — Dry to sweet amber fortified wine from the Jerez region of southern Spain or similar style wines produced elsewhere; usually drunk as an aperitif.

Shiraz — Also known as Syrah. A full bodied red wine made from a variety of grape cultivated in southern France, Australia, South Africa and the USA.

Slivovitz — A dry, colorless plum brandy.

Tokay — 1. A variety of white grape orginally grown near Tokaj (formerly Tokay), a town of eastern Hungary.

2. A wine made from this grape.

Van Der Hum — A South African liqueur flavored with mandarin orange.

Varietal — A wine made principally from one variety of grape, and carrying the name of that grape.

Vermouth — A sweet or dry fortified wine flavored with aromatic herbs and used chiefly in mixed drinks.

Vodka — An alcoholic liquor originally distilled from fermented wheat mash but now also made from a mash of rye, corn, or potatoes.

Whisky — 1. An alcoholic liquor distilled from grain, such as corn, rye, or barley and containing approximately 40 to 50 per cent ethyl alcohol by volume.

2. A drink of such liquor.

3. Whiskeys made in areas other than Scotland are spelled with an 'e' as in 'whiskey'.

INDEX

ACKNOWLEDGEMENTS

The publisher would like to thank the following people
who contributed to the supplies for the photoshoot:
Cecile Dragone
Donovan Hendricks of Trade Centre, Cape Town
Gareth Collins